Simple
TRUTHS
for an
Abundant
LIFE

MITT & ANN
ROMNEY

Simple
TRUTHS
for an
Abundant
LIFE

FROM ONE GENERATION
TO ANOTHER

DESERET
BOOK

SALT LAKE CITY, UTAH

All rights reserved. No part of this book may be reproduced in
any form or by any means without permission in writing from the
publisher, Deseret Book Company, at permissions@deseretbook
.com or PO Box 30178, Salt Lake City, Utah 84130. This work is not
an official publication of The Church of Jesus Christ of Latter-day
Saints. The views expressed herein are the responsibility of the
authors and do not necessarily represent the position of the
Church or of Deseret Book Company.

Deseret Book is a registered trademark of Deseret Book Company.

Visit us at deseretbook.com

Library of Congress Cataloging-in-Publication Data

(CIP on file)

ISBN 978-1-62972-590-1

Printed in the United States of America

Lake Book Manufacturing, Inc., Melrose Park, IL

10   9   8   7   6   5   4   3   2   1

To our grandchildren

CONTENTS

INTRODUCTION

This book began as a letter Ann and I wrote to our children, grandchildren, great-grandchildren, and distant descendants. After reading it, one of our sons felt that it might be of interest to other families, particularly those of our faith. He suggested that we offer it to the people at Deseret Book. We did.

Our letter follows in the tradition of the writings of many parents and grandparents of generations past. In recording their daily experiences and lessons learned in their journals and letters, they have passed on wise counsel and essential truths in hopes of guiding their posterity. As their words have allowed us and others to learn from the past, we hope that ours will build a bridge connecting to future generations.

To those who are reading this book, please forgive our references to immediate family events and personal experiences but know that while we may not be relatives, we are grateful to be connected with you as members of God's eternal family.

In some cases, we have changed names, places, or other specific details to honor the privacy of people we mention in this book.

And so,
our letter begins:

Dear Family,

If we have passed on before you were born, you do not know us but we believe that we know you. We love you. We anxiously await our meeting with you.

We decided to write this letter to share some of the lessons of our lifetimes. We have lived in interesting times and have enjoyed enormously varied experiences. Ann is a mother of five sons, a successful combatant against multiple sclerosis, an equestrian champion, a director of numerous charities, and a cofounder of the Ann Romney Center for Neurologic Research at Harvard Medical School and Brigham and Women's Hospital. Mitt is a father, the founder of a thriving business, and a senator, and has also been the president of an Olympic Winter Games, a governor, and the Republican nominee for president of the United States. Both of us have served in numerous ways in The Church of Jesus Christ of Latter-day Saints.

Fortunately, most of our life lessons have been passed on to you through your parents. But in case some of our stories or admonitions were omitted by them, we provide this supplement. It is not meant to be an in-depth treatise on everything we think you need to know, but rather a starting point of things to consider as you map out the life you want for yourself. We earnestly hope that you will read what we have written; it is our profound desire to connect with you even if you choose not to follow our advice. We also hope that you will seek out wisdom from others who have gone before you and shared their experiences along the way. We have learned that truth is not bound by time or place; you will surely find that wisdom from another's life, even from the distant past, can bring wisdom to yours.

Mitt is the English major in our partnership, so he has been the primary writer. The thoughts and counsel, however, are very much our mutual product—as are our descendants, we might add.

Ann Lois Davies Romney
Willard Mitt Romney

THE
FIVE
BIG
YEARS

In the era that Ann and I have lived, life expectancy has been about 80 years of age. Experts presume that this figure will rise to close to 100 in the future. Whether 80 years or 100, life lasts quite a while—though, as my father said when he was in his 80s,

"Anything that ends is short."

If we divide life up into five-year intervals, you will have 16 intervals of living on earth, assuming an 80-year life. During the first two intervals, much of what you experience is insular and, for the most part, forgotten. During the third interval—10 years of age until 15—your perspective and your choices will begin to expand.

It is the fourth interval, ages 15 to 20, that we call the Five Big Years. Decisions made during these years can impact all 60 that follow. Unfortunately, the very limited experience of people at this age, the arrival of powerful new hormones, the incomplete development of the brain, and the psychological neediness in these teenage years means that making wise choices is far from straightforward.

As grandparents, or perhaps distant ancestors, we offer our counsel regarding a few of the choices you will make. We have no dog in the fight you might be having with your parents or siblings; we are motivated solely by our desire for your happiness over your next 60 or 80 years. So here goes, first with some don'ts and then with some dos.

DON'TS

Don't get anywhere near substances that can become addictive.

Drugs, alcohol, tobacco, and probably other things that haven't yet been invented are powerfully attractive. Your friends may idolize people who do self-destructive things. Hollywood lionizes them. And, most enticingly, some of these things are extra-ordinarily pleasurable. But they have the power to be extremely destructive to your next 60+ years. They can enslave you. Try as you might, you may not be able to escape their hook. They may degrade your health and mental capacity. And they can become such a focus of your thoughts and desires that you lose the capacity to feel the joys and pleasures meant to come from things that provide lasting and fulfilling happiness, such as marriage, family, faith, friends, and career.

Don't get into pornography.

In any form. Looking at sexual material will release hormones into your bloodstream that provide a similar type of pleasure to drugs. As is the case with drugs, to keep getting the same rush, you will need ever more graphic and extreme stimuli. Porn is as addictive as any other compulsion. One problem with becoming hooked on pornography is that it will negatively affect your ability to experience a satisfying sexual relationship with your spouse. Sex is intended to strengthen the love between the two of you; if your sexual function has been distorted by porn, your ability to enjoy marital love—perhaps the greatest joy of your next 60+ years—will be impacted. Jesus, looking forward to latter days, said that "the love of many shall [become] cold" (Matthew 24:12). I am convinced that He saw the impact of porn and similar compulsions on our capacity to love.

Don't do things that can get you killed.

Dying young is a bummer. Taking risks is yet another way to pleasurably jolt your brain. Unfortunately, during the Five Big Years the judgment portion of your brain is not yet fully developed, and thus you do not yet adequately assess danger. So take our advice: get thrills and take risks if you'd like, but don't ever do unnecessary things that could end in your death.

Don't have sex before marriage.

As I said above, sex is an important element of a happy marriage. Much of its power to bind husband and wife comes from sharing it with only your spouse. The commitment Ann and I have to reserving intimacy for only each other is one of the reasons our marriage is so extraordinarily joyful. The profound, emotionally-charged sex of a committed marriage is worth waiting for. Gratefully, the Atonement of Jesus Christ makes it possible for everyone to become clean and whole, regardless of past choices. If you need to repent, do it, trusting that the Savior has the capacity to overcome all sin. In fact, He has already done so.

Besides the other negative effects these things bring, we note as well that premarital sex, porn, and drugs are incompatible with the presence of the Spirit. They make it much, much harder to find truth. Not only do these things alienate the Holy Ghost, but they confuse the mind and emotions; they will leave you vulnerable to making critical decisions that are harmful to your long-term happiness. If you have given in to any of these practices, please don't make any important, lasting life decisions. Give time, experience, and hopefully repentance a chance first.

DOS

Choose good friends.

Our friends from high school continue to be a part of our lives even to this day. We prized them then because they understood us, stuck by us, and defended us. We prize them now because of all we have experienced together. Friends and loved ones are the real currency of life.

Reach out to the outcast.

There are always a few kids who just can't catch a break. For whatever reason, they're cast aside by almost everyone else. The school award that we were most proud of was given to our oldest son: "To Tagg Romney, for Unselfish Concern for Others." Befriending the friendless can be a lifesaver for them and a character-builder for you. You will be surprised by how good it feels to make a difference in someone else's life.

Ignore the idiots.

You will undoubtedly be teased, bullied, or made fun of at some point. Peers will put you down, criticize you, and shun you. It's part of teen stupidity. Ignore it. If people are killing you on social media, don't read it. If you're getting harassed at school, try your best to keep your distance from the perpetrators. Reach out to adults who can help and support you. And, most importantly, recognize that the offenders are idiots. Whatever you are bullied for as a teen will become entirely irrelevant in your next 60 years. Tagg was so bullied that we finally put him in a different school. Today, he's a father of six, happily married, a bishop in the Church, a highly successful businessman, and he has a large circle of very tight friends. By contrast, the coolest guy in my high school—good-looking, star athlete, and all the girls' heartthrob—today is unhappy in a dead-end job and has an attitude of resentment over where he's ended up. High school is a terrible predictor of life.

Seriously consider going on a mission.

In the final years of this interval, you will decide whether or not to serve a mission. If the Spirit directs you to go, do it. It will change your life for the better. You will find God, if you have not already. My faith was pretty feeble when I faced this decision. I decided to go ahead largely because of my desire not to be the weak link in my family, because of my hope that the gospel was true, and because of the encouragement of my girlfriend, who was not even a member of the Church yet. She said that if I did not go, I would regret it for the rest of my life.

A mission will increase your faith in God. It will solidify your life priorities in favor of endeavors that bring the greatest happiness. It will enable you to feel the incomparable joy of bringing happiness to others you serve. You will enter friendships that will enrich the rest of your life. Missionaries I served with are among my closest friends even to this day. And people I taught are still in my heart; we regularly write and occasionally see each other when I am in France.

When I say that a mission will change your life, I'm also thinking of my cousin. Before his mission, he attended Princeton University. Spending his time playing sports and goofing around, he failed almost every class and was asked not to return. Then he served his mission. When he came home, he attended Florida State University, where he achieved nearly perfect grades and graduated at the top of his class. Things that mean a lot to you before a mission can look pretty meaningless after. A mission provides invaluable perspective on what will bring lasting happiness. If it's right, go.

If you read nothing else of our counsel, at least you'll have gotten some good basics from those dos and don'ts. But, of course, we do have just a bit more to share about the things that matter most, and we hope you'll read on.

GOD and CHURCH

Ann and I are entirely convinced that there is a God and that The Church of Jesus Christ of Latter-day Saints provides an accurate and truthful knowledge of our purpose on earth and the path to realize our potential hereafter. We are also convinced that

THE RESTORED GOSPEL OF JESUS CHRIST OFFERS THE ABSOLUTE BEST PRESCRIPTION FOR LIVING A FULL LIFE OF ABUNDANCE AND HAPPINESS.

That's quite a testimony, we know, but
we offer with it the process and reasoning
that led to our conclusions.

We acknowledge that faith in or testimony of these things is different from proof. If the existence of God or the truthfulness of His gospel could be proven with irrefutable fact and evidence, there would be no need for faith. And, as you know if you have studied the gospel of Jesus Christ, developing and growing faith is one of the primary purposes of life on earth. It was impossible to develop faith before this life when we lived in the physical presence of God because, well, He was right there before our eyes. So to be clear, the process that led to our conclusions about God and the gospel is not entirely based on unarguable evidence. But evidence there is. And it is abundant.

Our conviction regarding God and truth has three components: one spiritual, one experiential and one intellectual.

If you're serious about finding religious truth, all three components may be valuable.

The Spiritual

Before I went on my mission to France, I read the Book of Mormon, fasted for a day, and prayed to have God reveal to me whether it was true or false. Nothing happened. I had read in the book of Moroni that I would get an answer, and I assumed it would be clear, convincing, and probably somewhat physical. I had forgotten the earlier passages in the Book of Mormon that suggested that its truth could come instead through a more experiential, lengthy process (see Alma 32, for one example).

I hadn't received the answer I'd expected, but nevertheless I embarked on my mission, leaning on the faith of my parents, the tradition of my family, the weight of my ancestors' sacrifices for the Church, and the encouragement of my girlfriend, Ann.

The first year of my mission was seriously difficult: little success combined with mind-numbing repetition. But I studied a good deal and came to better understand the doctrine. My spiritual experiences were to follow.

While serving in the Paris district, living at 126 Rue du Château, I was ready to retire one evening when I was overcome with bleak and desperate feelings, almost as though a black cloud had enveloped me. Nothing like this had ever happened to me before. At one point, the thought even came into my mind that I should throw myself from the window of our fifth-floor apartment. Recognizing that these thoughts were not all my own, I remembered the account of Joseph Smith's First Vision, wherein he spoke of experiencing a similar bleakness.

So, thinking of his example,

I knelt down and prayed for deliverance.

Upon standing, I was filled with a remarkable sense of energy and clarity of thought. I spoke to my companion the words that came to my mind, including specific experiences that I felt would occur during my mission, the declaration that I would marry Ann and have many children, and a description of events and accomplishments that I could see occurring during my career. Of course, this all may seem to someone who did not experience it to be mere machinations of mind. But my words cannot capture the reality of what I experienced that evening. And nothing remotely similar has ever happened again. I am convinced that this was the influence of the Holy Ghost.

Several months later, while serving in Versailles, I received what might be called a spiritual gift. A Catholic priest, Père Chery, had advertised a lecture on "Mormonism" to be given at a local theater. The hall was packed. His attacks were well rehearsed and effective. The Berthelin family, whom we had been teaching, was in attendance. Mr. Berthelin was very negative about the Church and disputed my teaching. He was an engineer of some success, owning an ample single-family residence in Versailles. As the new district leader, it fell to me to do or say something about the priest's critical presentation. I stood at the side of the hall and began to refute each of his arguments. I was told by my companions afterward that my French had been flawless and my presentation superb. **Neither of those things was a regular occurrence, I assure you.** The priest tried to interrupt me, but the audience booed him and shouted for me to continue, which I did. Afterward, Mr. Berthelin came up to me and asked how soon he could be baptized. He later served in the district presidency.

As my mission proceeded, there were other instances when I detected the presence of the Holy

Spirit and was able to foresee people's behavior or take effective action. This was not an ever-present sense, however. The great majority of my mission was drudgery, sprinkled with flashes of clarity and exhilaration.

Spiritual experiences have attended my life since my mission as well. For example, Ann and I had decided that it did not make sense for me to run as a candidate for US Senate against incumbent Ted Kennedy in 1994. But while praying, I felt impressed to enter the race. That same day, Ann felt prompted that a campaign would be "like Zion's Camp." Ann didn't know what Zion's Camp was, but those were the words that had entered her mind. I explained that Zion's Camp had been a grueling journey taken by early Church members that accomplished nothing concrete, but also that those who had participated in it had been blessed with great faith and went on to serve in important ways in the future. So Ann and I had both received a clear answer. Interestingly, like Zion's Camp, my campaign couldn't exactly be called a success, but it led to the Olympics, the governorship, my nomination for president, and Ann's leadership in healing and research.

Many times, our prayerful requests for direction haven't been clearly answered even when pending decisions seemed important.

In such times,

Ann and I draw upon our best thinking and step forward with FAITH.

Ann's first spiritual experience regarding the gospel happened in 1965. On March 21 of that year, we had our first date: a premiere screening of *The Sound of Music* in Detroit. Weeks later, I was smitten, but Ann was unsure of how serious she felt about me. Her standoffish attitude may well have contributed to the aggressiveness of my pursuit. But by June, we both were in love.

Sometime that month, after a dinner date, I drove Ann to a hill near my parents' home with the intent of kissing. After parking the car, I was about to kiss her when she asked this question: "What do Mormons believe?"

This was definitely not the object I'd had in mind for the evening. But Ann persisted, and I, feeling some partial responsibility to share my faith, relented.

Ann's entreaty was the natural result of several months of inquiry about God that she had pursued with the minister of the church she and her family infrequently attended. She had particular interest in the nature of this supposed being, God. The minister described to her the Nicene image of God, that He was without "body, parts or passions" and that He was three personages in one: the Father, the Son, and the Holy Ghost. Ann was both confused and troubled by the minister's description.

My response to her question was of particular interest to her because I began my answer with the first article of faith, which I had learned in Primary as a child: "'We believe in God, the Eternal Father, and in His Son, Jesus Christ, and in the Holy Ghost.' Further, we believe that They are three separate and distinct personages. God and Jesus have physical bodies similar to ours, and the Holy Ghost has a body of spirit."

When I said these words, Ann was quite literally overwhelmed with a witness that I was speaking the truth. This confirmation was so intense that she broke down in tears.

The Spirit she felt was so undeniable and so penetrating that she has never questioned the truthfulness of the gospel since that day.

And throughout her life, Ann too has experienced many spiritual witnesses, each confirming her earliest conviction regarding God and His Church.

The Experiential

Alma 32 explains that if someone lives the gospel, and if doing so produces the happiness it purports to provide, that person has further evidence that the gospel is true. It is surely arguable that the gospel's prescription for happy living could merely be the result of scholarly analysis rather than divine revelation. Nevertheless, in combination with spiritual and intellectual evidences, this happiness is one more buttress for belief—particularly because the gospel's guidance for happiness is manifestly counter to conventional ideas.

For example, the gospel directs us to abstain from sexual relations prior to marriage, in part for our own happiness. A scholar might be more likely to claim that premarital sexual experience will improve sex during marriage and, of course, that having sex with multiple partners will be pleasurable along the way. My experience and research show that God is right and the experts are wrong. Depth of marital passion, fidelity in marriage, and the absence of divorce are correlated with chastity, not promiscuity.

The gospel teaches that children are a source of happiness. Society favors late marriage and few if any children. My experience confirms that children are indeed a primary source of life's meaning, purpose, and joy. Those who are in their early twenties and finding excitement in diverse activities may dispute my conclusion, but

DURING THE GREAT BULK OF ONE'S LIFE, CHILDREN AND GRANDCHILDREN ARE INDISPUTABLY A PRIME SOURCE OF HAPPINESS.

The gospel claims that alcohol, tobacco, and coffee are bad for your health. This claim was made well before science knew what we know today: tobacco is particularly threatening to health, and alcohol leads some people to become dangerously addicted. Coffee does not have known health risks other than its effect on sleep, but long and restful sleep is essential to maintain brain health, particularly in older people. The gospel got it right well before science confirmed it.

I submit that all the other gospel admonitions are also correlated with greater happiness. Consider the elevating feelings associated with serving others, honesty, humility, and generosity.

Going back to Alma, he also observed that a seed that bears good fruit must be a good seed. Because the gospel of Jesus Christ produces an abundant life—despite a skeptical world—its goodness and truth are likewise evidenced. For many people, the act of living the gospel—planting the seed, if you will—is how they first begin to find the truth.

The Intellectual

Numerous criticisms are levied against the truth of God and of our Church. Ann and I have studied a great number of these, and though some offer reasonable arguments, ultimately we have found them to be less than convincing. In every case, using a different perspective to consider the arguments has extinguished or diminished them. On the other hand, there are intellectual arguments *in favor* of belief that we find quite compelling.

One example is found in the witnesses of the Book of Mormon. These men claim to have seen the golden plates and, in some cases, to have seen the angel who delivered them. Had they all remained as leaders in the Church, their testimony could be written off as an agreement among themselves to profit from establishing a church that they would lead. But several of these individuals subsequently left the Church. Despite doing so, none ever recanted his sworn testimony. Some who left returned to full membership, but not leadership. If the witness of these many men had been falsely given, what benefit would they gain from continuing until their deaths to claim it was true?

The Book of Mormon itself is compelling intellectual evidence of God and the Church.

In fact, I wonder whether I would be a believer if we did not have the Book of Mormon. The Bible was written and compiled so very long ago and can be interpreted in so many different ways. If the Bible were our only evidence, I might have wondered why God had spoken so frequently to prophets of the past but had been silent for the last 2,000 years. I'm afraid that with only the Bible to rest my intellect upon, I may not have found sufficient substance for belief.

The Book of Mormon provides intellectual as well as spiritual basis for people like me. If you read it, you will recognize that **there is simply no conceivable way that it could have been written by a very young, uneducated man.** It is far too lengthy and complex, too consistent with obscure biblical references, too obviously written by different writers, and too wise to have been dictated from thin air by a mere boy. It could be argued that Joseph Smith was reading from a text that someone else had written, or perhaps that he had written it over several years. But witnesses of his dictation report that he simply looked into a seer stone—usually placed inside a small hat—as he spoke to the scribes, who wrote down his words. He was not turning pages. There is no logical explanation other than that the words came from God, as Joseph said.

Over the years, my faith in God has also been reinforced by certain scientific realities. But these are less compelling to me than the evidence within the Book of Mormon. And, because science has a way of eventually finding explanations for things that once seemed inexplicable, I don't place a great deal of weight on them. Still, there are some that may be worth mentioning for the intellectually curious.

Two examples come to mind. First, the fact that there is only one liquid that expands when it becomes a solid: water to ice. Were this not so, the surface of the ocean, the portion that freezes in the winter, would sink to the bottom, eventually forming layer upon layer of ice, which, of course, would never thaw. Only a shallow ocean at the surface would thaw and freeze with the seasons. Marine life, and probably all complex organisms, would be impossible. A Creator, not chance, is responsible for this singular reality.

Second, I'm far outside my zone of expertise here, but I can report that matter and anti-matter should have been produced in exactly equal proportions with the Big Bang, and that if that had been so, the universe would not exist. Who but the Creator could have tipped the equation to enable the Creation?

Of course, some contend that science *disproves* the existence of God. That's a bridge too far, of course. Science may ultimately prove that a god was not required to create the universe, but it cannot prove that God does not exist. Nevertheless, some point to certain scientific facts that religion is unable to explain as evidence for disbelief.

We believe that true science and true religion are entirely consistent.

If a religion asserts that a scientific fact is wrong, and then if that scientific fact is ultimately proven beyond reasonable objection (the existence of dinosaurs, for example), I'm inclined to believe that the religion—or its spokesperson—was simply wrong.

Dinosaurs did exist. Obviously. True religion has no problem with that. God created the earth and allowed natural physical laws to populate it with living creatures. One of these laws is evolution. Dinosaurs evolved according to natural law but were ultimately eliminated, perhaps as an act of God. Ultimately the creatures we see today evolved over the millennia. And when, through evolution, the humanoid creature became sufficiently like the image of God, He gave it the spirit that made it what we are today. That's science and gospel according to the Book of Mitt—not necessarily gospel, of course, but possible. There are many, many possibilities that harmonize supposed conflicts between true religion and true science.

An Entreaty to Believe

If you study and serve as we have studied and served, we believe you will come to have faith in God and in The Church of Jesus Christ of Latter-day Saints. But as an incentive to choose to study and live in faith, let us offer a few more thoughts.

Belief in God will give your life purpose beyond yourself, which is a key element of a happy life.

Further, it will provide you and your children with concrete answers to life's questions; you will escape the vacillation that leads to uncertainty and stress. Order and boundaries and certainties are psychologically necessary and beneficial. Belief in the Church provides them.

The Church's teachings and guidance are enhanced by the conviction that the individuals who lead the Church are inspired and directed by God. Accordingly, guidance can always be current through revelation and is therefore relevant to changing global circumstances and individual needs. **The benefits of being a faithful disciple of Christ that will come in the next life are of a wholly different magnitude.**

Membership in the Church has several very beneficial byproducts. The community of members is an antidote to solitude, a shelter in the inevitable storms of life, a psychological and temporal safety net, an incomparable support in raising children and teens, a source of meaningful opportunities for genuine service, a training school for leadership, and a source of engagement and activity at every stage of life. Read that list again, slowly, and with thought about each benefit. So far as we have been able to determine, participation in no other organization, religious or otherwise, is as encompassing, supportive, and rewarding as active membership in The Church of Jesus Christ of Latter-day Saints.

Each of the aforementioned benefits applies to our lives while on earth.

Even if your faith in Christ is based on mere hope, the eternal rewards of living in accordance with His gospel justify your effort. Quite simply, you will be able to live in the presence of God and Jesus, remain bound to your spouse and family, gain knowledge of all things, and participate in the creation of future worlds. All this and more. It is undoubtedly a worthwhile endeavor to unceasingly seek God and to live the gospel.

CHARACTER

The ultimate example of great character is Jesus Christ. Model yourself after Him, and you will fulfill the measure of your creation. Even when you fall short, aiming to become more like Him keeps you on a path of noble character. Similar examples are found in the lives of the prophets. Studying the Master and His disciples in the scriptures provides an incomparable guide for a successful, abundant life.

If Ann would indulge me for a moment to write directly about her:

I am constantly inspired by Ann's Christlike attributes. She told me just recently that one of the things she thinks about in every place she lives or in every endeavor she undertakes is whether she has left people better for her having been there. In her words, **"DID I LEAVE FLOWERS AND GOODNESS IN MY WAKE?"**

After she told me this, I gave her ambition some thought. In fact, she has indeed uplifted the lives of others in every setting I could think of. She has taught young people from the scriptures in early-morning seminary classes; she has redirected United Way toward more productive, faith-based charities; she has shared her struggle with disease through her books and personal counseling; she has founded a center for disease research; and she has nurtured and led by example in our family to help both me and our sons become better people. I had not previously realized that she had made a conscious effort to improve lives on every path she walked—including my life. It has made quite a difference.

Whether through the example of the Savior and His disciples or that of the good people in our lives, we have come to understand the merit of developing certain aspects of our character. I share two of those with you here.

Trust

I decided early in my life that I would keep my word and honor my promises even when subsequent circumstances made it disadvantageous for me to do so.

Of course, it is only when disadvantageous circumstances arise that honoring a promise means something. I made a promise to pay 10 percent of my gross income to my church. In the first year of our financial prosperity, that number was so large that I could easily have rationalized reducing the percent or only applying it to our net income. Ann cried when I gave the bishop our large check. I asked her why the tears; she said she was so very happy to be able to give so much. I joked that I was crying for a different reason!

I know quite a few people who honor a promise just until their self-interest becomes large enough to break it. They then concoct an elaborate justification for abandoning their word. I am convinced that their rationalization is entirely subconscious; they would be incensed at any suggestion that they were going back on their word. But with such individuals, a pattern of repeatedly backing away from commitments develops. I worked with a business partner who agreed to split an investment 50–50. When the opportunity began to look more profitable than we had expected, he decided that he needed at least 60 percent, explaining that it was taking more of his time than he had originally planned. I walked away from the investment, giving him all 100 percent; I never wanted to do business with someone who didn't keep his word.

As in business, things in politics must work on trust. Without it, negotiations are impossible. As governor, I met each week with the two legislative leaders of the opposition party. Our mutual understanding was that the discussions we had were private. We often spoke of matters that had potentially damaging political implications for one side or the other. But not once in our four years was the trust abused. I saw these men as political adversaries, but I also saw them as men of character.

YOU WANT TO BE A PERSON WHO CAN BE TRUSTED. While we believe a reputation for trustworthiness will enhance your career, there is no guarantee that it will do so. On the flip side, one very wealthy businessman-turned-politician I know well made many millions despite a reputation for regularly reneging on contracts and commitments.

Whether or not being **TRUSTWORTHY** will win in business, it will result in a **satisfied mind** and a **clear conscience.**

Integrity

I once attended a business seminar led by two psychologists. As a teaching exercise, they asked us to write down the names of the five people, living or dead, we most admired. I decided to choose people from different parts of life: Jesus Christ, Abraham Lincoln, my father, Ann, and David O. McKay. They then asked us to write down the three qualities we most associated with each one of these individuals. Accordingly, I now had a list of 15 attributes. Finally, they said to identify the two or three words that appeared most frequently on our lists. Mine were love, honor, and service.

These three qualities, they explained, were our "core values." Further, the psychologists asserted that if we conducted our lives in a way that was not consistent with these values, we would experience stress. That stress would harm our health, impair our relationships with others, and make us unhappy. If our conduct conformed with our values—if, in other words, there was integrity between our conduct and our values—we would have greater satisfaction and happiness.

I can't certify the methodology of this exercise, but I am convinced that it led to a truth. Most of us are far from having lived in complete harmony with the values we most admire, but we can earnestly try to do so. The result will be that we don't look back on our lives with regret. Of course, there are specific instances in my life I do regret; interestingly, the ones I remember are times when I veered away from my fundamental values.

Consider what qualities you most admire, and endeavor to conduct your life in a way that is consistent with them.

A LIFE OF INTEGRITY IS ITS OWN REWARD.

MARRIAGE

On a topic as important as this, you'd think we would have ample counsel. Not so. Our marriage was and is so unusual that we don't think our experience will be a very helpful guide.

You'll see why.

We fell in love young—very young. I was in my senior year of high school, 18 years old. I had dated several of Ann's friends. In each case, I had been an ardent suitor right until the point when the girl began to reciprocate my interest. Then my ardor inexplicably disappeared, and I was on to the next.

At a party at a friend's home, I met Ann. She was the most beautiful and interesting young woman I had ever met. Where she had been before that night, I don't know. She was almost 16 and had never really dated. I gave her a ride home, explaining to the guy who had brought her that I was doing him a favor because I lived close to her.

Our first date was a week or so later, on March 21, 1965. As I mentioned earlier, we went to downtown Detroit to see *The Sound of Music*. After I drove Ann home, we kissed.

I assumed she was now my steady. **She felt no such thing.** When she subsequently went to a school dance with Greg Dearth—as I was recuperating from appendicitis—I was both jealous and upset. She was incensed that I was so possessive. Interestingly, the more uninterested she seemed, the more I pursued her. Within a few weeks, however, she expressed feelings like my own. At the junior prom in June, we told each other that we were in love. I proposed, and she accepted. Crazy, I know. But there has never been a question about our love since.

It would be four years before we could marry. I was away at Stanford for my freshman year of college and then two and a half years on my mission in France. At Stanford, I got a job as a shuttle driver to make enough money to occasionally fly home to see Ann. While I was in France, she dropped by on her way to a BYU semester abroad in Grenoble (the rules were a little more lax back then).

When I returned home from my mission in December of 1968, Ann was waiting for me at the airport with my family. Of course, she was the first person I embraced. On the drive home, she and I sat in the third row of my sister's Oldsmobile Vista Cruiser station wagon, out of earshot of the family. During the four years I had been away, Ann had of course dated other guys—some pretty seriously. A few had actually proposed. And I had been gone so long that I had wondered how intense my feelings would still be.

But as we huddled in the back of that car, it was as if we had never been apart.

Right then and there, we decided to get married as soon as possible. Our parents held off the marriage until March.

We were married on March 21, 1969, four years to the day from our first date.

Conflict

Our fifty years of marriage have seen children, grand-children, Ann's multiple sclerosis, my prostate cancer, extensive travel for work, election victories and defeats, Church assignments, equestrian competitions, Ann's neurological research center, and much more. Through it all, we've never had a fight. Really. We know, crazy again.

We can't explain why we never fight. Of course, we've had disagreements. We've had hurt feelings. We've had to apologize to each other now and then. But no fights. This is why our marriage advice is so limited.

What accounts for this? Not having to struggle with money problems surely helped. When I was about 10, my dad invested my $2,000 savings from birthday and Christmas gifts in American Motors stock, which subsequently went from $7 per share to over $90 per share. This would pay for college and graduate school tuition, as well as living expenses so long as we were frugal. Our Provo apartment was $62.50 a month, and our weekly grocery budget was $13. Do the math, and you can see that even adjusting for inflation, we were careful with our money. My first salary of $30k per year was more than ample; subsequent jobs at higher salaries meant that we would always have enough and to spare. So unlike many marriages, we had no conflicts over money and spending.

Our values, opinions, and expectations were very similar, perhaps because we had almost grown up together, belonged to the same church, went to the same schools, and were raised in the same small town. Agreeing on most things surely reduces marital conflict.

It also helped that we quickly learned not to let our exhaustion after a long day exacerbate conflict. **Things can get pretty distorted at the end of the day.** We found that we tended to blow matters way out of proportion when we were tired. Sometimes, speaking together in bed, in the dark, we would become so riled up about something that we could hardly fall asleep. When we woke up the next morning, we wondered why we had been so upset the night before.

My parents' marital advice was that you should never go to sleep mad. Given our experience with nighttime irrationality, I'd suggest the opposite:

If you're unhappy with your spouse as you're heading to bed, sleep on it until morning when things will be back in perspective.

Overall, our sources of conflict were pretty minimal. At the same time, we did things that brought us closer together.

Sharing

Nights were good times for us to talk, particularly when the boys had gone to bed. We each made the effort to truly understand what the other's day involved. In our early years, much of our talk was about Ann's day at home with the boys. We confided in each other and counseled together about the best ways to teach and raise our sons. We spent a very great deal of time talking about each boy, every single day.

Ann was interested in what I was doing at work and sympathized with the slights and challenges I experienced there, offering valuable insights and perspectives for me to consider. Years later, after she was diagnosed with multiple sclerosis, Ann took up riding horses and equestrian competitions. **This wasn't naturally a subject I was drawn to, but because it was important to her, I made sure it became more important to me.** Funny thing: as I became more knowledgeable about the sport, it became more interesting to me.

Having interest in your spouse's occupation, daily activities, and interests is a huge part of communicating that you love her or him. You show your interest by devoting meaningful time to talking about those things and, where feasible, participating in them together. When our boys were young, Ann was of necessity a full-time mom, staying home with them each day. When I came home, I put my work away entirely. The briefcase stayed closed. While I was at home, I strived to devote every minute to Ann and the boys.

One of my sons told me that almost every day, he asks himself what he can do to make his wife happy. It may simply be expressing gratitude for a thoughtful idea she has shared, complimenting a meal she has prepared, or praising her management of their finances. Just as important, it also means things that take more time, like going to an event she would like to attend, taking a vacation to the place that she—not he—prefers, spending time with her parents and siblings, and so forth. Whether or not this is a daily consideration, it is a principle of marriage we believe is essential to a happy marriage: consciously and regularly doing things that your spouse likes even when you do not.

You will be happiest
in your marriage
if you are giving more
of yourself to your
spouse.

Marriage is about giving and sacrificing.
It comes naturally with your love, and it
will make your love even stronger.

Sex

The advice columnist Ann Landers was once asked whether in her decades of providing marital counsel she had ever heard of a troubled married couple that was also experiencing "great sex." She replied that to her astonishment, she had not. Without belaboring the correlation problem with her data, I'll just add that physical intimacy is a huge part of a loving, happy marriage. A marriage professor explained to me that hormones released during intimacy tend to psychologically draw two people together, making their mate seem even more attractive. I also believe that we men attach a good deal of our self-esteem to marital intimacy. Whatever the reason(s) might be, sex is a very important part of marriage, and thus not to be trifled with. It is a critical component of a happy marriage, and not just for the early years.

A related point: infidelity is a marriage killer. Take every step you can to avoid any circumstance that might lead you to become emotionally or physically involved with someone other than your spouse.

Ann and I have always made an effort to be attractive to each other and to have self-confidence. Exercise and healthy eating have kept us more vibrant. Making efforts in our health and grooming in order to be attractive to our spouse is one way we show we appreciate and value each other — and ourselves.

Loyalty

Stand by your spouse. Only a couple years after we were married, it became pretty obvious that Ann's mom resented me: Ann was an angel, and I was an unworthy male interloper. When we were back home for Christmas, I walked on eggshells. Even so, I got the cold shoulder. One afternoon, Ann decided to take the bull by the horns. She confronted her mother, forcefully told her that her behavior toward me was unacceptable, and said that if it continued we would leave the house and not come back. Eavesdropping in the hall, I was all smiles. And oh yes, her mom straightened up.

It's harder to defend your spouse when he or she is wrong, of course, but that's when it counts the most. On occasion, I would come home and recount how I had been unfairly criticized or disrespected at work. Ann always saw things my way. In time, I recognized that in fact I might have sometimes deserved what had come my way at work. Ann was wise enough to realize that it was better for me to come to this conclusion on my own than for her to point it out.

Fixing Your Partner

There are few things more treacherous than trying to get your spouse to change. We recommend embarking on such an errand only if absolutely necessary. One of our nephews and his wife drove across the country shortly after their marriage. To pass time, they decided to tell each other one physical thing they would change in the other if they could (a very, very bad idea). She said that she wished his legs weren't so short and stubby. Countering, he said that he wished her breasts were larger. Years later, they still tell the painful story.

But encouraging change in areas of import may be necessary, perhaps even critical to the marriage.

Don't believe the maxim that people can't change.

We can when we must.

One thing I needed to correct was that when we were out with friends, I sometimes didn't show Ann the kind of respect she deserved, interrupting her or monopolizing the conversation. This she expressed openly to me in car rides home. I argued defensively at first, but she didn't back down. It took a while, but I learned to become more aware of her participation in conversations and of my overbearing tendencies. I changed.

I know of one acquaintance who has an anger problem. When something sets him off at home, he yells—quite abusively at times. His wife demanded that he control his temper; it was corroding the love she felt for him, and the marriage was in peril. He insisted that his temper was an inherited trait he could not control and could not change. She asked, "Do you ever lose your temper at work or with your clients?" Thinking, he realized that no, he had never lost his temper in a work setting. Her point hit home: he *could* control his temper if he had to, but at home he had felt that he could get away with not doing so. He changed.

If something really needs to change, tell your partner before it festers.

Expect defensiveness, argument, denial, and even a bit of rejection, but these things will pass. Get the problem remedied so that your love isn't damaged.

On the other hand,

if you'd like something to change but it's not a big deal, maybe just let it slide.

The maxim "what you first abhor, you then endure and eventually embrace" can apply to those little irritants that come with living with another person you happen to love.

RAISING
A FAMILY

During our early marriage years, the greatest disparity between conventional thinking and the teachings of the Church was whether or not to have children, and particularly whether to have more than one or two. The Church followed the counsel of the Bible, which said, "Children are an heritage of the Lord: . . . Happy is the man that hath his quiver full of them" (Psalm 127:3, 5). Popular thinking at the time was that having children put a strain on the environment and risked the world running out of food and water. When Ann told her dad by telephone that she was pregnant with our third child, her father hung up on her. (To her father's credit, when Josh finally arrived, her dad's heart was softened and he embraced him. He also welcomed sons four and five.)

When our sons were young marrieds, the impetus for not having children had changed. Now the thinking was that children kept you from having and doing all the things you really liked. Children would be a constraint on buying things and on simply being able to do what you want when you want. We had friends who told us they were going to buy a dog to see whether they wanted a child. Really.

There's no question about it: children do in fact take over a big part of your life. They constrain all manner of activities and absorb your money. At the same time, they are the best thing, by far, that will ever happen to a husband and wife. **Nothing compares.**

I've never met someone who said that they wished they hadn't had children. I'm sure there are some people out there who feel that way, just not normal people. I remember asking my dad what the greatest accomplishment of his life was. Let me remind you that he had run a major automobile manufacturer, made millions of dollars, become a three-term governor, run for president, and served in a president's cabinet. His answer: "Raising the four of you kids." I would give everything I have and everything I have done to save one of my children or grandchildren from pain and suffering. Having things and having children aren't even in the same universe of happiness.

The Rewards of Challenges

One of the things that makes children so wonderful is that they are often a nightmare.

We know, that sounds nuts. But the greater the effort involved in something, the greater the satisfaction in seeing it succeed. If it were easy to raise a child, the sense of achievement and fulfillment would not be nearly so great.

And yes, children can be an enormous challenge. Health worries and accident scares accompany the early years. For the most part, however, these years are enormously joyful. The tween years are further compensation for the terrible teen years ahead. Teenagers make bad decisions, take unnecessary risks, ignore the counsel of parents, and often delight in doing whatever they have discovered bothers you most. Our son Matt has said that as a teen he learned what buttons he could push to drive his mother over the edge. Tagg was disgusted with me for a host of reasons, from my chewing too loudly to my wearing pants with legs that were slightly too short. The next three sons were so appalled by the antics of their two older brothers that they went pretty easy on us. Fortunately, the terrible teens last but a few years. Boys become men, girls become women, and marriage and grandchildren follow. Glorious.

But the path does not always end so wonderfully. Teens can make choices that set them on a collision course. We know of no action, no curriculum that parents can follow that is guaranteed to prevent an unhappy outcome. We have watched superb parents follow wise and inspired counsel to the letter and nevertheless see one or more of their children go off course, sometimes seriously. Whether it be the children of prophets, apostles, presidents, doctors, or psychologists—no calling, no training, no expertise can entirely prevent a young person from making bad choices. Each child is an independent person, free to make his or her own decisions.

That doesn't mean that following counsel, sacrificing, and seeking inspiration are ineffective. We have found that these things make an enormous difference. Parents who faithfully do these things will see all or almost all their children embrace provident life choices—if not immediately, then eventually.

Consider what you are trying to accomplish as parents.

At the most basic level, we all hope to keep our children from behaviors that almost everyone agrees are self-destructive: abusing drugs, alcohol, and tobacco; dropping out of school; taking mortal risks; and so on. These were never really a problem with our sons; our advice on preventing these is thus of limited value. We spoke about drugs a good deal around the dinner table, noting how stupid it would be to try them. Maybe that was sufficient. Attending school was so obviously the path required to live a successful life that our kids never considered dropping out. Most fortunately, their friends felt the same way about these basics; that was probably more important than anything we said.

Instilling Values

The next level of parenting is a good deal more challenging: imbuing your kids with your values, particularly if your values are different from those of most other people. Some of our friends have said that they didn't try to do this, that they let their children "find themselves" and find their own values. I guess if you don't mind your children choosing Hollywood's values, or the values of other teenagers, or the values of the gym teacher, then that could work fine. But if you hope your child will embrace values more elevated than those, expecting a child to find these by him or herself is folly. They spend hours and hours every day experiencing the values of society at large, in school, in media, in video games, and in the locker room.

Instilling distinctive values requires a campaign that is purposeful, thoughtful, determined, and loving.

Distinctive values and choices we wanted for our sons included total honesty, service to others, kindness, faith in God, appreciating hard work, observing the law of chastity, respecting all people, willfully attending religious instruction and worship services, and serving a mission. The full list is a good deal longer, but you get the picture: we hoped our sons would have very different values from society at large.

Leaders of our Church have prescribed several things to imbue children with these values, such as regular church attendance, a family night once a week, family prayers every day, prayers before meals, and daily family scripture reading. Attending church every week went without saying for us. Ann and I were less regular with family night. We blessed the food regularly. Family prayers were hit or miss. I wish I had been better at all of these. Even though we were far from perfect in following our Church leaders' counsel, we used each teaching occasion as an opportunity. Kids' minds are pretty open in the years leading up to their teens. Steadfastly teaching them during those years can help carry them through the hormonal years.

In addition to the Church's prescribed counsel above, we found several strategies that we believe make a difference in passing on your values to your children.

One of these was automatic. I once asked a renowned child development psychologist what the most important thing Ann and I could do to raise good kids was. His answer: "Love each other." Parents who love each other have an enormously positive effect on their children.

Another child psychologist had advice on discipline. He said that there are three types of parental discipline approaches. The first, "brick-wall parents," insist that their children do everything exactly as they are told. A directive from one of these parents might go this way: "Go back upstairs and iron that wrinkly shirt right now!" Then there are "blade-of-grass parents." They lie flat and let their children run right over them. Finally come the ones that do the best: **THE "REED PARENTS." LIKE THE REEDS NEAR A POND, THEY HAVE BOTH STIFFNESS AND FLEXIBILITY.**

They draw a line on important things but let lesser things go.

Such balance is easier said than done, of course. It is hard to tell when you are being too strict or too easy.

Honestly, we were never cut out to be brick-wall parents. The (false) image of the perfect Latter-day Saint family with a sparkling house and children nestled in bed right on time wasn't something we ever considered. Our boys were ever fighting, ever making crude sounds and smells, and generally making us laugh uncontrollably. One Saturday evening session of stake conference, the visiting speaker was Elder Dean L. Larsen of the Presidency of the Seventy. I was serving as stake president at the time, so I was seated on the stand, and Ann was sitting in the congregation. As was tradition at the time, Elder Larsen would spend the night at our home after the meeting.

During his remarks, Elder Larsen said that he learned a great deal about a stake president's home life when he went there after the meetings. In well-run homes, he explained, the children were in their pajamas waiting quietly for family prayers. In other homes, chaos. At that moment, Ann stood up in her seat and abruptly left the room. The congregation burst into laughter; they knew she was rushing home to get our little troublemakers into their pajamas and quieted down before Elder Larsen would arrive. When he and I eventually got home, it was a scene out of a Norman Rockwell painting. Ann and I have laughed about it for about thirty years.

The value of hard work is taught only one way that we know of: **working side by side with your children.**

Saturdays were chore days at our house. Our ample lawn was cut by our sons. They weeded the flower-beds. When it snowed, we shoveled together. In this, I was simply following in my father's footsteps; as a boy I mowed the lawn, weeded, watered shrubs and trees, and shoveled the driveway with my dad. I now know he could easily have paid for someone else to do these chores, but he instead saw them as a vital way to teach me to work. Summer jobs can also help. Our boys worked as waiters, ice cream scoopers, landscapers, and ranch hands.

Racism and misogyny are learned behaviors. So are respect for others, inclusiveness, and recognizing that all people are children of God. We made sure that our sons heard us express our profound feelings about these things. I recounted to them that I pulled off the road and cried with joy when I heard on the radio in 1978 that all worthy males, of all races, were to receive the priesthood. We also brought our boys with us as we served or socialized with people different from ourselves.

Keeping Children on the Path

If you wish, as we did, to have your children live the gospel and serve missions, your own words and devotion will be most important. We have found that in active Latter-day Saint homes where one or both of the parents criticize the Church or its leaders in front of their children, about half of those kids end up leaving the Church, compared to only one in five in homes where the parents do not. It seems to us that children are especially tuned to hear their parents' conversations—particularly criticisms. Adults may understand these criticisms in the context of their faith, but children, apparently, do not.

CHILDREN ARE INFLUENCED BY HEARING THEIR PARENTS PRAY.

Do their parents sound like they really believed they are talking to God, or is it more like empty words said into the air? Do their parents bear testimony in church and at home? Do they love the scriptures, the temple, their Church leaders? And do they live during the week like they act at church on Sunday? Parental hypocrisy is a near guarantee of a child's estrangement from the Church.

It would be wonderful if you could choose your children's friends. During teen years, friends may have more influence on your children than you do as parents. Trying to steer your teens away from someone sometimes makes them more, not less, inclined to spend time with that person. The best strategy we found was to

CREATE AS MANY OCCASIONS AS POSSIBLE FOR OUR SONS TO BE TOGETHER WITH PEOPLE WHO SHARED OUR VALUES.

So in addition to church and early morning seminary, it meant youth campouts with church groups, appropriate social events, sports programs, and youth gatherings at our home.

Sabbath observance was a hard thing for us to define. Some parents prohibit their children from playing on Sunday, from watching TV, and from using social media. We presume that works well for them. Ann and I wanted our kids to look forward to Sunday, not to dread it. And we were afraid that too strict observance would cause them to rebel. At the same time, we wanted the day to be significantly different than a Saturday. So we red-lined some activities but not all fun. Our rule was no swimming, no going out to the movies, and no commercial activity on Sunday, but things like watching TV, playing catch, or hiking were okay. Interestingly, our sons as parents are generally stricter about Sabbath observance than we were. Maybe we were too lax.

Some of you will raise your children in a non-traditional family, perhaps as a single parent. Your job will undoubtedly be a good deal more difficult without someone to give you a break when you're at the end of your rope, someone to strategize with you, and someone of the opposite gender to serve as a role model. We aren't expert on your challenge; we can only imagine that if we had been similarly situated, we would have wanted to find other adults who could help fill these roles. My sister became a single parent; always seeking spiritual guidance, she raised four very faithful and impressive children.

Individual Needs

One of the peculiar challenges of raising kids is that they are so very different from one another. We had five boys, each drawing from an identical gene pool, and yet each remarkably distinct from the other. One responded best to a pretty tight rein; another rebelled at any reins at all. Part of parenting is deciphering the differences and adjusting accordingly. Like many parents, we were probably too controlling on our first and too lax on our last. One thing that each responded to, however, was love.

One day, we had reached the end of our rope with one of our teens. I dragged him into the kitchen and sat him down, hard, on a stool. He looked at Ann and me like we were the most hated people on the planet. His words matched his look. I don't remember what it was that had set him off, but whatever it was, he wanted nothing more to do with us. He wanted out. My inclination was to give as good as I got. Had he been seven, I would have probably spanked him. Since he was seventeen, my words would have to be my weapon. As I readied myself to launch into him,

an unexpected thought

came into my mind:

tell him

how much you

love him.

Where had that come from?!

But that's just what I did. And Ann joined right in with me. We went on at some length, not just professing our love but expressing why it was that we loved him so very much. As we watched, he began to soften. He listened intently, accepting our expressions. And then we began to actually communicate with each other.

Another son had emotionally turbulent teen years. His mood swings and emotional heights and lows were well beyond what we had experienced with our other sons. We tried every approach we could think of, but nothing seemed to dampen his frustrations and resentment. One evening as Ann sat in contemplation, two realizations came to her mind. First, **God loved this boy as much as she did,** and second, God was surely the best child psychologist in the universe. So she prayed to know what He would have her do, and she followed the promptings she felt. Several times a week, she would go into this son's room after dark and sit by his bed. With lights out and darkness to cover their emotions, they would talk about his experiences of the day. As he began to feel less alone, more confident, and more loved, his temperament smoothed.

Our daughter-in-law Jen related that she found it almost impossible to reach her daughter during her daughter's late teen years. Everything Jen said, every effort she made to connect was met with an audible sigh and a quick exit to her room. The singular response to her entreaties at dinner was, "Whatever." So Jen decided to write her daughter a letter expressing her thoughts and to place it on her daughter's bed. This she did week after week for more than a year. Her daughter never acknowledged seeing or reading the letters. But Jen kept writing them nonetheless.

Years later, home from a mission, this daughter told Jen that she had not only read those letters when they appeared in her room, but she had also taken them with her on her mission. She reread them time and again. They had profoundly influenced her, stabilized her, and given her confidence.

You will undoubtedly find that parenting through the teen years has unique CHALLENGES.

Unique creativity

and unflagging effort

may be part of the

SOLUTION.

If you have the opportunity and health to have a child, do it. Children stretch the spirit and educate the mind. We are convinced that for many of you, they will be part of living a life in full.

TRAGEDY
and TRIAL

Some of you will pass through life without any serious trial. Others will endure tragic loss. Over our lifetimes, we have endeavored to understand why some are afflicted and others are not. Of course, those who embark on destructive or improvident paths are subject to inevitable consequences. But even those who choose wisely are not immune from the trials of mortal life. We are convinced that living the gospel of Jesus Christ will bring you happiness. That does not mean, however, that you will be spared from tragedy. It is not possible for us to calculate the relative incidence of tragic loss for faithful Latter-day Saints versus others, but our personal observation is that there is little difference. If there were a marked, significant escape from pain for disciples, there would be long lines at church doors. And further, the need for a test of faith would disappear. Yes, I believe that God does intervene in certain circumstances, but it is the exception, not the rule.

EXPECT LOSS,

SICKNESS, AND PAIN.

They are part of

mortal life, not the

consequence for

something you

have done.

At church one day, a speaker described his experience with loss and what he had learned. He served as a seminary teacher, and both he and his wife are very faithful members. Their first pregnancy resulted in a stillbirth. Four years of infertility followed. Finally, a little girl blessed their lives. When she was two and a half years old, she developed a cold. Her doctor checked her out and found nothing unusual. The next morning, she lay dead in her little bed.

In the years that followed, two scriptures in particular touched this man's heart. In the book of Job, God explains that when the host of heaven heard His plan for a mortal world, they shouted for joy (see Job 38:7). This they did knowing full well that they would be subject to pain and tragedy like that which had befallen the man's little child. Thus, knowing eyes then in heaven had seen joy, even though we here now on earth see only the suffering.

The second scripture recounted Thomas thrusting his hand into the resurrected Christ's wounded side and feeling the wounds in His hands (see John 20:27). Interestingly, this man noted, Christ had risen from the dead with His wounds. Spiritually, we too will rise with the wounds of our lives having made us who we are.

THERE IS
PURPOSE,
EVEN IN
TRAGEDY.

EARNED
SUCCESS

Arthur Brooks, one of the most impressive social psychologists of our time, explained that "earned success" is one of the keys to happiness. By using the term "earned," he noted that inheriting money or position doesn't actually make someone happy;

We need to feel that we have achieved success through our own effort.

What is meant by "success" is a larger topic. I think most people measure success in terms of material wealth or position. If they obtain at least as much wealth and stature as they had expected, they feel that they have been successful. Those expectations are influenced by the material achievement of their parents, their friends, and their community, and increasingly by what they see in media.

Ann and I were impressed by the extraordinarily happy demeanor of the people we spent time with on some of the poorest islands in Indonesia. Their impoverished homes and nonexistent opportunities met their extremely limited expectations. Likewise, psychologists have concluded that the people of Latin America are a good deal happier than their much richer neighbors in the United States. Meeting low expectations makes people happier than missing high expectations, even when the latter still results in a much higher level of material success.

To some degree, you will inevitably measure your success by comparing your material accomplishments to those of your parents and others. Perhaps this is why so many children of very wealthy parents are unhappy: they cannot meet the outsized expectations.

Luck of the Draw

One problem with this is that it is not at all certain that you will have greater material wealth and stature than your parents or your associates. I say this not because of any inferior ability you might have but because material wealth and promotion are subject to serendipity—to luck, so to speak. It is simply not true that brains and hard work will make you rich and famous. There are way too many factors that are out of your control.

When you read about people who became rich or famous, their path may seem obvious in retrospect—almost foreordained. But you generally don't read about the many, many other people of equal or greater ability who did not become either wealthy or notable. Often, the reason for the disparity in outcomes is a matter nobody could have foreseen. I say this as someone who became richer and more famous than I would ever have imagined; Ann and I know firsthand that a great deal of our success was the result of things we neither did nor planned.

Brains, **education**, **hard work**, and **wise decisions** were necessary, but they were far from sufficient: **good fortune** was also necessary.

*We say to our sons that we
"won the lottery" to underscore
that luck had a big role in our
material success.*

We want you to be happy. We also know that I can't do much to influence your material expectations. But we want you to understand that material wealth and secular achievement are not the most important measures of success. As you look back on your life, as we have now done, you will realize that your relationship with your spouse, the love of your children, your faith in God, your personal character, and the closeness of your friends—these are what bring the greatest happiness. They are the real wealth of your life. Success in these ways means you have lived a truly successful life.

Note that success with family, friends, and faith are almost entirely under your control: they are not subject to luck. So if you use these factors to define yourself and to gauge your success, your happiness will be almost entirely within your hands.

With that in mind, clearly our prior counsel about marriage, children, and faith is the most relevant for guiding your success in life. We do, nevertheless, have a few thoughts regarding your career and work.

Ann's Career

By deciding to have five sons in ten years, Ann made being a full-time homemaker her career choice. At the time, much of society demeaned the roles of motherhood and homemaking. While many of Ann's friends at church had made the same choice she had, neighbors and friends outside the Church looked down on her. Still aspiring to make the most of her intellectual gifts, she attended night classes at Harvard. Sometimes she had to bring a nursing baby along, and she couldn't help but notice the dismissive looks from other students.

Her job at home was harder than mine at the office. Much harder. It was also more important than mine. And **our work raising children has brought us greater happiness than anything I have done in formal employment.**

Some years after I graduated from business school, Ann and I were invited by a professor at Harvard Business School to participate on a panel to discuss our career choices. The husbands and wives of the other two couples on the panel were professional lawyers or investment bankers. As they spoke, Ann wondered how the class would respond to her uncommon career.

She explained that her career required an extraordinarily broad group of skills: she had to be a psychologist, an educator, a medical diagnostician, a coach, a chef, a chauffeur, a counselor, and an expert in practically every subject at the boys' schools. She noted that her hours were longer than mine, that personal breaks were out of the question, and that she received no direct financial compensation. She concluded by saying that she believed she had the best career in the world, with rewards that were incalculably large.

Silence for several seconds. Then, a standing ovation.

The reality of our world today is that most of you will not become full-time homemakers and parents. Many of you will not have financial circumstances that even allow it. But if you feel called to the work of being home with your children, explore thoroughly how it might be possible before you dismiss it. Ann was a highly accomplished mother, and it made for her a thoroughly fulfilling career.

After the boys left the nest, she was able to pursue another career, to the extent that her multiple sclerosis made that feasible. She took on a key role in a United Way charity, then competed in equestrian dressage, then championed the Ann Romney Center for Neurologic Research. And from my point of view, one of her most valuable careers was as my long-term advisor and counselor. Every decision, every strategy, every initiative I undertook was made only after deliberation with and advice from her.

We have been **lifelong partners** in **politics, business,** and **homemaking.**

Mitt's Career

I hoped to someday run a car company, like my dad. One summer during my graduate school years, I worked at Chrysler Corporation. While I liked the people I worked with, I was dismayed by the enormous distance between people like myself and anything interesting or important. I got a dose of bureaucracy, and I didn't like it.

A summer job at the Boston Consulting Group led to my employment there after graduate school. Later, I would join Bain and Company. In consulting, I learned concepts and techniques not taught in business school. I worked on important problems, and I enjoyed the work. Finding new sources of information, analyzing, applying concepts, finding answers, and enabling implementation were my bread and butter—literally and figuratively.

My boss, Bill Bain, approached me one day with a proposal: leave consulting to create a venture capital and private equity firm. Characteristically, we studied the industry for almost a year, concluding— incorrectly—that it had peaked. I signed on anyway.

We established operating principles: **abide by the highest standards of integrity**, **put the interests of our investors above our own**, and **have fun**. The team members we brought on were brilliant and wonderful people. They are close friends even now, twenty years after I left the company.

With funds entrusted to us by endowments and individuals, we invested in companies we believed we could help succeed. Often, our investments were leveraged with debt. Here is where luck came in: during the next 15 years, the stock market went from about 1,000 to 10,000 points. Only an idiot could lose money in such an environment, and we were not idiots. We made more money than I would have ever believed possible.

I left the company in 1999 to lead
the Salt Lake Winter Olympics.
Ann convinced me that

I WOULD NEVER BE

HAPPY IF ALL I DID

WAS MAKE MONEY;

I HAD TO MAKE

A DIFFERENCE.

We saw the Olympics as a demonstration of the great qualities of the human spirit. It turned out that Salt Lake City had bribed officials to secure the Games. When the truth came out, the Salt Lake Olympics were in jeopardy of failing. And so my turnaround experience was needed.

I also had some relevant public relations experience. As mentioned earlier, in 1994, I had run for Senate against Ted Kennedy. I knew that I had almost no chance of winning, but I believed someone needed to point out that his policies were hurting the poor and hurting America. I lost by 20 points. But I gained experience that would later serve me well.

The Olympics were a great success thanks to a great team. Afterward, I expected to go back into business, but an entreaty by the Republican Party Chairman of Massachusetts convinced me I was needed as governor. Success there led to two bids for president of the United States and to winning the Republican nomination in 2012.

Never in my wildest dreams could I have predicted such a disjointed career path. Doors were opened that I would never have foreseen. Some events propelled my successes, and others weighed it down. But there's not a single decision I would take back. Each was an adventure, an education, and a source of enduring friendships.

Your Career

What's all this got to do with you? A few observations: it is nearly impossible to see where decisions will lead you, even though it is still important to evaluate each choice as thoroughly as you can.

PRAYER
was a part of every important decision.

Sometimes an answer was clear; other times Ann and I proceeded in faith following the best thinking we could do.

We never put family and faith in the back seat. Some people justify giving these things short shrift by rationalizing that when they make more money, they will have more time for them. Baloney. By the time they make all that money—even if they do—their family and faith will have drifted away. The price of putting career and money before family and faith is incalculable.

About politics, consider the advice my father gave me: "Politics is about service; only go into politics if your kids are raised, you can pay your mortgage without winning an election, and you have something important to contribute." I never imagined that I would get into politics, because I never thought I would be financially independent. Dain Capital made that possible. My experience and values convinced me that it was an obligation.

My dad had another piece of career advice that has stuck with me: "**If you want to succeed, do your present job well.**" If you spend your energy looking for the next job, giving less than your all in your current job, that next job is far less likely to ever come along. And just as important, **doing any job well is a source of satisfaction**. All jobs have dignity.

A LIFE OF
Abundance

Borrowing from a familiar aphorism, life is wasted on the living. For spirits awaiting their turn on earth and for spirits who have left it, life surely must seem an exquisitely glorious and precious thing. Perhaps we the living take it too much for granted, sometimes letting it glide by almost without a thought.

As our years have brought us greater perspective and as the setting sun on the horizon is nearing, our appreciation for the magnificence of life grows.

We have written this letter

hoping it may help you

EXPERIENCE AS MUCH OF THE GLORY OF LIFE AS IS POSSIBLE.

We look back with appreciation for parents and wise teachers of all kinds who guided us toward the choices that made our lives unimaginably abundant: marriage, children, faith, friends, purpose greater than self, character, and the path of gospel living. May your lives be full to the brim.